JIMMY EVANS

Steps to
SEXUAL
FULFILLMENT
IN MARRIAGE

Family and Marriage Today™
P.O. Box 8400
Amarillo, TX 79114

All examples in this book involving ministry situations are real. However, the details and surrounding circumstances may have been altered or combined to preserve the privacy and confidentiality of the individuals involved.

For simplicity, the masculine pronoun is used when speaking in general terms; it is intended to be interchangeable with the feminine.

All Scripture quotations are from the New King James Version (NKJV), copyright © 1979, 1980, 1982, Thomas Nelson, Inc., Publishers, unless otherwise noted.

The Keys to Sexual Fulfillment In Marriage
ISBN 0-9647435-6-6
10 9 8 7 6 5 4 3 2 1
Printed in the United States of America.

God created the institution of marriage, as recorded in the second chapter of Genesis. He created it in a paradise called "Eden," meaning "pleasure and delights." From the very beginning, God designed marriage to be an intimate union between a man and a woman that would be filled and fueled by sexual pleasure and delight. We must remember that sex is God's creation and that His desire is for us to enjoy it to its fullest within the parameters of marriage.

We must also remember that all of the Scriptural prohibitions against sexual sins and perversions are not given by God to keep us from having fun or being fulfilled. Every warning from God concerning sex in marriage is to keep us from destruction. God's motive is love, not legalism. Even though many people in our society boast of their "sexual freedoms" as they violate the warnings of Scripture, their lives prove the fact that the penalty of sin is still death.

We live in a sexually permissive society marked by rampant sexually transmitted diseases, adultery, broken relationships, broken hearts, and broken dreams. These devastating effects of sexual sin are what God is trying to keep us from experiencing when He warns us about certain types of sexual behavior. His moral commandments aren't meant to spoil our sexual pleasure. They are safeguards to ensure that our sexual fun and fulfillment can last for a lifetime in a secure and growing relationship.

Even though the fallen world and the devil try to accuse God and His Word as being anti-sex, we must remember that God created sex, and He is the One who made it so exciting and pleasurable. This is a very important truth for us to understand and accept. If we don't understand this, we are set up to be deceived into believing that we must visit the realm of sin to really experience sexual pleasure and fulfillment. This is a common deception, and there are even many Christians who believe it. In counseling over the years, I can't count the number of couples I have seen who have ended up devastated or divorced because one or both of them crossed the line sexually and ended up paying a huge price. Their road to ruin began with believing the common deception that God's sexual parameters are unfair and that sexual sin would enhance their lives without negative results.

The truth is, sex in marriage is wonderful. God wants us to enjoy it to its fullest. Many people wonder if a truly spiritual person should think about sex and enjoy it without reservation. Again, this is the type of thinking the devil loves and wants us to accept. He wants us to believe that if we are good Christians, we just won't be very sexual. This is the opposite of the truth. God created us with a threefold nature: body, soul, and spirit. Being spiritual doesn't mean we deny reality or the inherent nature God created within us. It means that we turn every area of our lives to the lordship of Christ and fulfill His desire for us.

God's desire for our bodies is that we be blessed and fulfilled. This includes the area of sex. God isn't so cruel that He would give us a desire and then frustrate it. God is a good God. He creates beautiful things and wants us to enjoy them. Marriage was the first institution God created. In His original design of marriage in Genesis chapter two, God created Adam and Eve with a beautiful nakedness in a paradise of pleasure. They were created by God to enjoy sex in an intimate marriage relationship. Sin, not God, ruined Eden and caused Adam and Eve to fall from God's perfect plan.

Today, sin and deception are still causing people to forfeit the beauty and pleasure of sexual fulfillment in marriage available to all of us. If we will simply accept the fact that God loves us and wants us to enjoy sex for the rest of our lives within the parameters of a committed marriage, we can begin to experience true and lasting sexual fulfillment. This is the reason I am writing this booklet. I want to help you experience God's best for your life and marriage in the area of sex. I also want to help you avoid some of the common pitfalls and problems of sex in marriage.

Therefore, in the remainder of this booklet, I will explain three important keys to help you experience sexual fulfillment in marriage.

KEY #1

*UNDERSTAND THE SEXUAL
DIFFERENCES BETWEEN
MEN AND WOMEN*

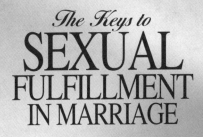

The Keys to
SEXUAL
FULFILLMENT
IN MARRIAGE

When Karen and I first got married, I was completely ignorant concerning the inherent sexual differences between us. In addition to my ignorance, I had also been deceived by pornography, locker room lies, and media portrayals of sex. I was a sexual problem waiting for a place to happen. Therefore, when Karen and I married, even though we were attracted to each other and had an active sex life, there was a great deal of frustration on both sides because of wrong sexual expectations.

It took years before we finally understood our differences and began to respect them. As we grew in understanding and respect of our differences, our sexual intimacy and pleasure grew dramatically. No longer were we placing unrealistic expectations on each other or expecting one another to act in a way outside of our natures. Here are some of the important things we learned that can help you succeed in sexually relating to your spouse:

a.) <u>Men are visually stimulated, and women are emotionally stimulated</u>. Women are by no means blind as it relates to sex, but they have a much greater capacity for responding to emotional stimulation. This is hard for men to understand. Because of this, many men don't take the time to talk to their wives and patiently meet their emotional and romantic needs. This lack of emotional support costs men dearly in the area of sex.

Every man must realize that his wife isn't going to turn on sexually just because he takes his clothes off. Women turn on because their husbands talk to them throughout the day and pay attention to them. Women rarely respond to sex beyond the state of their emotions. This doesn't mean that a woman can't give herself to her husband sexually if she doesn't feel like it. It simply means that her emotional nature is an integral part of her sexuality.

In understanding why God made women like this, we must understand that God is concerned about the overall integrity of the relationship, not just about sex. Therefore,

God designed sex in marriage to reach its potential only if genuine care and sensitivity are present. The opposite of this is the common scenario of a selfish husband ignoring his wife until bedtime and then expecting his emotionally impoverished wife to perform sexually. In His divine genius, God created a system that ensures that jerks don't get good sex.

The best sex in the world is achieved by respecting the differences in our spouses. Concerning women, this means that a man cares for his wife in a sensitive and sacrificial manner. This includes the all-important ingredient of romance, which simply means that a husband initiates behavior that pursues and pleases his wife on her level of need and desire. When a husband does this, his wife becomes sexually open and responsive to him.

Concerning a man's sexual nature, men are very visual. Even though women may have a problem understanding this, it is an undeniable fact. To fulfill her husband's sexual desires, a woman must realize that he can become aroused very quickly simply by looking at her. Because women are much more critical of their own bodies and don't respond visually as much as men, they have a tendency to discount this issue and therefore frustrate their husbands' need.

Women need to realize that their husbands want to see their naked bodies. Even though flannel nightgowns and pitch-black bedrooms are the sexual refuge for many women who don't want to expose themselves, they are the archenemy of sexual fulfillment for men. Just as a man needs to understand and meet his wife's emotional needs, a woman must respect and fulfill her husband's visual needs. This means going outside of her comfort zone to wear attractive lingerie before sex and to expose her body to her husband before and during sex for his satisfaction.

To understand the differences between men and women in the area of sex, all you need to do is look at how they sin. Men turn to pornography that wrongfully feeds their visual need, and women turn to soap operas and romance novels that wrongfully feed their emotional need. Rather than pursuing fulfillment sinfully outside of the relationship with our spouses, we must learn to respect each other's differences and meet each other's needs.

b.) <u>Men need sexual touching, and women need non-sexual affection</u>. This issue is one of the most confusing differences in men and women. When we don't understand this basic difference between us, sex becomes a bittersweet battle of wills. The common scenario that is played out in countless bedrooms is an aggressive husband roughly groping his wife's genitals as she complains and retreats into a sexually defensive posture. The result is their needs are denied, and they both end up frustrated.

To be fulfilled in sex, men must understand that their wives need soft, non-sexual touching throughout the day and during sex. This is a deep need for a woman. It makes her feel valued and emotionally cared for. The more soft, non-sexual affection a man gives his wife, the more sexually responsive she becomes. This is the opposite of the way a man is designed and thinks. That is why most men think that the way to turn their wives on is the way they are turned on – by direct sexual touching. This is wrong and leads to sexual frustration rather than fulfillment.

On the other hand, women need to understand that their husbands desire direct sexual touching. It is very satisfying and stimulating for a man, and it meets a deep need in him. Therefore, when husbands and wives understand each other and respect their differing natures, their times of intimacy will involve an affectionate husband caressing and gently touching his wife as his wife touches his penis and the areas of his body that are sexually stimulated.

Obviously, as sexual intensity builds, a woman needs direct stimulation to her clitoris to be able to reach orgasm. There are a number of ways this can be achieved, but it must be done in a tender manner that satisfies her desire and doesn't ignore her overall need for soft, non-sexual affection. There also may be other areas of a wife's body she wants her husband to touch and caress, such as her breasts. However, it must be done in a manner that is pleasing to her.

The most dangerous element that threatens sexual fulfillment is selfishness. When couples refuse to accept their sexual differences, they ensure that they will both be frustrated and not fulfilled. The best sex is achieved when both spouses are trying hard to meet each other's needs. Two sexually sensitive and selfless people are the ones who reach sexual fulfillment in their marriage.

c.) <u>Men and women have different levels of sexual need and achieve orgasms differently</u>. The majority of men are more sexual than their wives. This means they think about sex more and have a more intense need for it more often. This is especially true among younger men between 18 and 45 years of age.

As women age, their desire for sex often increases. Some of this is because of a greater emotional security in their marriages. Also, the absence of the fear of pregnancy and/or a greater acceptance of their sexuality can cause women to become more sexually open.

As men age, their testosterone level gradually drops, which causes a decrease in sexual desire. This change usually begins to be noticed as a man is in his forties or fifties. Therefore, throughout the life of a marriage, it is possible for either spouse to desire sex more often, less often, or the same amount as the other. Seldom will their desires be exactly the same. In general, it is the man who desires sex more than his wife, but I have counseled many a frustrated wife whose husband was disinterested in sex.

The main point in saying all of this is to illustrate the need for us to be accepting of each other, even though we don't always have the same sexual intensity or need at the same time. It is devastating for either a husband or a wife to be judged, ignored, or rejected by a spouse when expressing a sexual need. Our needs are an inherent part of us. Therefore, when we reject our spouses' needs, we reject them.

I'll never forget the young couple I counseled who were on the verge of splitting up. The crux of their problem was that she was put out by his regular need for sex. As I listened to him tell his side of the story, I heard a normal young husband expressing his desire for sex with his wife, and the rejection and shame he felt from her. As I listened to his wife tell her side of the story, I heard her saying that she didn't accept his sexuality. She fully expected that he would rarely need sex. As a result, she flatly rejected his advances as she accused him of being perverted for wanting so much sex.

Regardless of how much shame or rejection couples heap upon each other, sex is a deep need, especially in men. When this need is understood and accepted, good will and intimacy are shared between a man and woman. When it is misunderstood and rejected, serious problems and sexual frustration result.

The next step in accepting how we differ in our sexual responsiveness is understanding how men and women achieve orgasms. Men must achieve orgasm to experience sexual fulfillment. However, women can have sex with their husbands without experiencing an orgasm and still be satisfied. This is difficult for most men to understand, but it is nevertheless true.

Men almost always achieve orgasm during intercourse, and women rarely do. Even though it is possible for a woman to experience orgasm during intercourse, it is difficult because a woman's primary sexual organ that produces an orgasm is her clitoris, and it is located outside and above her vagina. Therefore, a woman needs to be stimulated on her clitoris to be able to achieve orgasm. Even though she can enjoy sex without an orgasm, most women desire orgasms on a regular basis. When a woman has the desire to achieve an orgasm, she needs to express this to her husband and guide him to stimulate her properly.

For a husband to meet his wife's need to

achieve an orgasm, he must slow down, be gentle and listen to her. Some men selfishly rush into sex and only care about getting their own needs met. The result is that their wives feel used and sexually frustrated. Men must understand that women warm up to sex more slowly. They require attention before, during, and after sex in order to experience sexual fulfillment.

Men can become sexually aroused almost instantly. Therefore, men can try to rush their wives into a sexual response that they are unable to give without the proper care. As I heard Gary Smalley say, "In the world of sex, men are microwave ovens and women are crock pots." This is a universal truth. Regardless of how men are sexually wired, they must realize that their wives are different and require the proper attention and care before and during sex to reach their potential.

This doesn't mean that all sex in marriage has to be experienced in the same manner. Some sex in marriage can be satisfying through "quickies." This usually means that a spouse (most often a wife) offers her body to her partner for the sake of meeting an immediate sexual need. A "quickie" simply means that through intercourse or some other means, sex is achieved in a more spontaneous and timely manner.

However, for a woman to reach an orgasm and to experience full sexual satisfaction, a "quickie" won't suffice. Women need to be romanced and cared for before sex. During sex, a woman needs foreplay, affection, loving communication, and the stimulation of her clitoris in a manner that pleases her. In this way, a woman is able to reach an orgasm and be sexually satisfied.

As stated, men and women are very different sexually. Understanding these differences and respecting our spouses' sexual nature leads to sexual fulfillment.

ELIMINATE THE COMMON ENEMIES OF SEXUAL FULFILLMENT

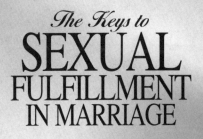

The Keys to
SEXUAL
FULFILLMENT
IN MARRIAGE

If couples are going to experience sexual satisfaction for a lifetime, they must properly respond to some common problems that can sabotage their hopes for success. Even though all of these problems can be overcome, they must be taken seriously and addressed properly. Sadly, many couples who marry with great sexual energy and attraction between them end up fighting or even divorcing, citing their sexual problems as the primary reason.

Because sexual problems are one of the main reasons for tension between married couples, I will address three common enemies of sexual fulfillment, and how you can overcome them:

a.) <u>Unresolved anger</u>. Anger is inevitable in every marriage. There is no way two people can live together without becoming angry at each other at some point. Even healthy couples can experience anger on a regular basis. This may surprise you, but it's true. The issue isn't whether we will experience anger; the issue is how we deal with it.

I have counseled many couples over the years who experienced sexual problems. A good number of them were experiencing sexual difficulties as a result of unresolved anger between them. There is a direct connection between our emotions and our sexual responses. When we are resolving issues in our marriages successfully, our sex lives are unhindered as we express our physical love. However, when issues remain unresolved and anger builds, our sexual desires and responses change. I believe unresolved anger is the most dangerous element in marriage.

It is critical for husbands and wives to be honest about their emotions and to allow honesty from each other. It is also essential to deal with anger quickly. The Apostle Paul in Ephesians 4:26 tells us to admit our anger, but not to let the sun go down on it. Sexual health isn't just an issue of how our bodies respond to sexual stimuli. It is very much dependent upon our emotional state. Unresolved anger means there are feelings of hurt, mistrust, or violation between us. The more these issues accumulate and remain unresolved, the more it will be reflected in our sexual responses.

Sex acts as both a thermometer and thermostat in a marriage. As a thermostat, sex makes marriage better. Good sex actually increases the emotional temperature of the marriage and builds feelings of intimacy and goodwill. However, it also acts as a thermometer, which means it reflects the state of the relationship. Sexual problems can many times be due to unresolved conflict. A lack of healthy sexuality between a couple for any significant length of time is a warning signal that could be reflecting unresolved anger.

If you have unresolved anger in your marriage, I would recommend that you be honest and allow your spouse to be honest. Talk about your feelings as you commit to forgive your spouse and not to allow anger and bitterness to remain. If you can't resolve an issue or issues between you, get counseling from a Christian leader or professional. Your marriage is too important to allow problems to remain unresolved. It is robbing you of the intimacy and pleasure every married couple can and should experience.

b.) <u>Stress</u>. We all know that we live in a fast-paced culture. One of the most common problems resulting from stress is sexual inhibition. The demands of jobs, children, housework, financial pressures, and other issues can leave one or both spouses exhausted and sexually unresponsive. This isn't a problem if it happens infrequently. However, when it happens regularly, it can create deep frustration for the spouse whose sexual needs are being ignored.

The first thing we must do to remove stress from our lives is to prioritize. Regardless of what some people may think, you can't have it all. Life must be prioritized to be successful, and every priority must be protected from competing demands.

God created marriage to be the highest priority in life with the exception of our personal relationship with Him. He expressed this clearly in Genesis 2:24, where He stated that a man would have to leave his father and mother in order to be joined to his wife. This means that the highest priority in life (the blood bond between ourselves and our parents) must become a lesser priority for the sake of marriage.

Taking an inventory of our lives is necessary on a regular basis, especially when we are experiencing stress. As we do, we need to examine those things that demand of us physically, emotionally, and mentally. If we realize that the greater priorities of our lives (God, marriage, children) are being robbed of their rightful place by lesser things (friends, work, sports, hobbies, entertainment), we must be willing to reprioritize or even remove the lesser things.

Earlier in our marriage, I gave up golf for several years because of this very issue. I have always loved to play golf, but earlier in our marriage, it was an idol. I would go directly from work to the golf course and then come home exhausted and unwilling to meet Karen's needs. However, I expected her to serve me and meet my sexual needs. She was deeply resentful, and it became a major issue in our marriage. Giving up golf was a sacrifice for me, but as I look back, it was a small price to pay for the incredible intimacy we have today.

It doesn't matter how successful you are at work or how much money you have if you aren't happy at home. If you think about it, you will agree that nothing in life has the potential of making you as happy or as miserable as your marriage. Because of this, it is worthy of the highest level of sacrifice and investment. Make a decision to prioritize your marriage first and to make whatever sacrifices or changes are necessary to give your spouse the time and energy he or she deserves.

Another common issue of stress relates to children and housework. For any husband wanting good sex, he must assume the responsibility to help with the kids and the home. It is unfair for a man to come home from work and to sit in front of the television, expecting his wife to bear the burden of children and housework and then to come to bed exhausted but willing to energetically meet his needs.

Regardless of whether a woman works outside of the home or at home, a husband needs to let his wife know that he is her partner in every area of life. A wise husband who wants to enjoy good sex will bear the burdens for his wife and allow her to have a time of rest and relaxation before sex. An unwise husband will ignore his wife and refuse to accept responsibility for the home, children, finances, or other issues that are causing her stress.

In dealing with the common stresses of life, it is also a good idea to plan sex in advance. This certainly doesn't prevent spontaneous sex; it just means making a special date for sex on regular occasions so we can both prepare properly. When our children were young and we had many demands on us, this is what we did. We would decide in advance to have an evening together and make it happen.

These were always great times because we prioritized and planned for them. Also, every two or three months, we would go for a night or two to a motel or hotel just to be alone together. When I look back on our marriage and how we succeeded in very busy times, I believe this was a key reason. We didn't let circumstances dictate to us; we prioritized being together and enjoying sex, and we made it happen.

One other issue related to stress: Children are under stress more than ever, and it directly affects us as parents. Just like adults, many children believe they have to have everything and be everywhere. If their demands and desires aren't monitored by wise parents, children will end up being driven through life with their parents as the "chauffeurs." Even though every parent will have to work and sacrifice for their children, common sense should tell us where proper parameters should be established. I know many couples whose relationships have been damaged and even destroyed because of the unrestrained demands of their children.

c.) <u>Deception</u>. The world we live in is filled with sexual deception. We are surrounded by it every day, and if we aren't careful, it will infect our thinking and sabotage our marriages. Today, men are being deceived by pornography. A man need not leave his home to be confronted daily with erotic images from television, magazines, computers, and movies.

Little, if any, of the erotic imagery around us is consistent with Scriptural truth. Satan, in his desire to destroy us, attacks us with his flaming missiles of deception. Pornography is satan's special weapon to destroy men and marriage. It is nothing less than satanic sex education.

Pornography portrays women as sex objects without emotional needs. Therefore, as a man views pornography, he is led to believe that "normal women" want sex as much as he does and in exactly the way he does. This inevitably leads him to believe that there is something wrong with his wife and that he is being robbed. I have seen many men abuse and abandon their wives as a direct result of the deception of pornography. As men, we must realize that pornography is a lie that leads us into deception and bondage.

The more pornography a man views, the more he must see to satisfy the ever-increasing need it creates. Also, the more pornography a man views, the raunchier it must be to satisfy him. Worse still, as a man escalates in his pornography addiction, he will eventually want to act out what he is seeing. He will often try to use his wife in his acting out, which dehumanizes her and makes her nothing less than an object of vaginal masturbation for him. Or, worse still, he will go outside of his marriage to try to experience the lie of pornography.

God has designed sex to be satisfying only if it includes intimacy. Intimacy means an inner closeness and depth of relationship that includes body, soul, and spirit. Therefore, sex in marriage is the only sex that can satisfy because it draws from all of our experiences and areas of life together. Pornography bypasses every other area of life and promises sexual fulfillment solely on a physical level.

This is the essence of the lie of pornography. I have known men who have destroyed their lives in the pursuit of illicit sexual pleasure. They are driven to constantly feed the monster of sexual excitement, but with ever-diminishing levels of satisfaction. Their ruined lives are the end result of the deception of pornography.

Many women are also being deceived related to sex. Romance novels, soap operas, movies, Internet chat rooms, Web sites, and female erotica all court a woman's differing sexual temperament. Again, though we rarely see them as such, they are all forms of satanic sex education.

Let me use romance novels as an example. They are almost always written by women and for women. Romance novels portray reality in the opposite manner as male-oriented pornography. They excite women by downplaying the sexual nature of men and "over-emotionalizing" them. Because they are written by women and for women, they swing to the sexual perspective of women and ignore the reality of the sexual intensity of men. The worst result of romance novels and female erotica is that they convince women that there are men out there (unlike their husbands) who are much more emotional and much less sexual. The danger is that a deceived perspective is deeply implanted in women that many times causes them to judge and reject their husbands as they convince themselves they are losing out on "true love."

As husbands and wives, we must reject the lies of the devil and refuse to be entertained or excited by them. As we do this, we must realize the truth about sex. It is only fulfilling as we both turn our hearts to each other and work hard to meet each other's differing needs. We are created sexually different, and great damage is done to our marriages when we reject those differences and try to conform our spouses into our image. This is exactly what pornography and female erotica do and why they are so dangerous.

KEY #3

*WORK TO CREATE
AN ATMOSPHERE OF
SEXUAL PLEASURE*

The Keys to
SEXUAL
FULFILLMENT
IN MARRIAGE

Once you understand the differences in your spouse and how to disarm the common obstacles to sexual fulfillment, you can pursue unhindered pleasure. This is one of the greatest blessings of life and marriage. We are sexual beings, and without a doubt, sex is the greatest physical pleasure in life. As I said at the beginning of this booklet, God created marriage in a paradise called "Eden," meaning "pleasure and delights." In doing so, God clearly revealed His design and desire for marriage—that it would be a place of sexual pleasure and delight.

Even though virtually every married couple engages in sexual intercourse, not every couple experiences the same level or frequency of pleasure. Couples can greatly enhance the degree of sexual pleasure in their marriages by creating a favorable atmosphere. Here are four ingredients that create an atmosphere of sexual fulfillment and pleasure:

a.) <u>Give attention to physical health and proper grooming</u>. There are two dangerous extremes in our society today related to our bodies and sex. One extreme is the drive for physical perfection, which causes many people to go to unhealthy extremes to try to make themselves more attractive. It also means more people are demanding unrealistic physical standards of their spouses. I recently counseled a couple who were separated and on the verge of divorce. The husband constantly criticized his wife for her weight. She was three pounds over her ideal weight. Not only were his standards unrealistic, he constantly compared her with women's bodies he saw in magazines and on television. She felt rejected and overwhelmed.

Another extreme is when people abuse their health without regard to how it affects their spouses and their sexual relationship. Whether it is heavy drinking, drug abuse, or obesity, these issues directly affect our sexuality and our marriages. Therefore, we must accept responsibility to take care of ourselves. Sexual performance is directly affected by our health. The older we get, the more this is true.

Beyond the issue of health are the issues of hygiene and grooming. A man should be sure that he is clean and doesn't approach his wife with dirty hands, etc. Also, the trimming of nose hair and ear hair, having clean teeth and good breath, bathing, using cologne, being clean-shaven, and dressing well are all important factors. If we want our wives to be attracted to us and open themselves up to us sexually, we must understand how important it is to them that we care for ourselves. To our wives, the way we groom ourselves is a true measure of how much we care about them and how much we are willing to invest into the relationship.

For a woman, grooming means that she cares for her hair, dress, and overall appearance. I recently saw a woman who was attractive and well-kept before she married, but immediately afterward she "fell apart." I see her and her husband regularly, and it is obvious that she is taking him for granted. The standard she used for her appearance before their wedding dropped immediately afterward.

Even though her husband is visually stimulated, her disregard for her appearance is in truth a disregard for his needs. Poor grooming and hygiene are dangerous ingredients that create a negative sexual environment. On the other hand, caring for our health and grooming adds a powerful dynamic to a positive sexual atmosphere.

b.) <u>Communicate honestly and openly about your sexual needs and desires</u>. The only way we can truly know how to please our spouses sexually is for them to tell us. This can and should happen before, during, and after sex. This type of communication happens as we both commit to sharing and to receiving what is shared. It is also important that we create an atmosphere in which our spouses feel comfortable sharing their sexual needs and desires without being rejected or condemned.

Obviously, if our spouses share something with us that is sinful or violates our conscience, we don't have to accept it. However, even if it is sinful and violates us, we must be careful how we respond. We need to let our spouses know that we still love them and are committed to them sexually. This is something women deal with a lot. Some husbands want their wives to do something that violates them. It is important for a woman to be true to her conscience without damaging the relationship with her husband or communicating rejection.

On the other hand, many men become frustrated with their wives because they only communicate with them sexually through negatives. In other words, rather than openly sharing their desires and what pleases them, their wives reserve their sexual comments for when they are doing something wrong. "Stop!" "Don't do that!" "That hurts!" "I don't like that!" Those kinds of comments are the only instruction some men receive to guide them in trying to please their wives. This is not only frustrating, but it is also confusing and counterproductive.

Almost every man I know wants to please his wife sexually. This doesn't mean that men don't have their own problems. It just means that most men desire to please their wives, but they depend on positive instruction to succeed. This is especially important because men and women are so different in their emotional and physical design and desires. A positive sexual environment must include communication that creates a clear roadmap that leads husbands and wives to fulfill their spouses' sexual desires.

Concerning this issue, there is another important point that can hinder healthy communication. Some people, especially women, are raised with repressive attitudes concerning sex. It is usually communicated through a parent's sexual comments and attitudes. If parents view sex in a negative light, they will normally transmit this directly or indirectly to their children. The effects can be profound upon a child's future sexual relationship with a spouse.

Again, I want to emphasize the point that God created sex and that it is beautiful. God's perfect will is for you to have a pleasurable and exciting sex life with your spouse. Don't be ashamed of sex or treat it as a taboo issue. Talk about your sexual desires, and encourage your spouse to do the same. Don't let the devil rob you of the joy of sex by making it a dirty subject. Sex is God's property, and it is one of the greatest blessings in life. This is the proper way to understand it.

Also, some people view sex in a negative light because of a sexual sin or practice of their pasts. If you've done something wrong, you need to repent and receive God's forgiveness. But don't let the mistakes of your past keep you from succeeding today. Sex, just like anything else, can be good or bad. Use your past as a reminder of what you shouldn't do. Let God's Word be your guide of what you should do. If you're wondering what the Bible has to say about sexual pleasure, you can begin by reading the book of the "Song of Solomon." Get ready to be surprised at how vividly the Bible describes sexual intimacy in marriage.

Also, many people, especially women,

have experienced sexual abuse in their past. In some cases, this abuse is extreme. Without exposing the sexual abuse to the Lord and allowing Him to heal you, your sexual health and marriage can be affected in a negative way. It is imperative that you get help if necessary and deal with previous abuse if it is keeping you from opening yourself to sexual pleasure in marriage. There is nothing that God can't heal or give you the power to overcome.

c.) <u>Use creativity and energy in giving sexual pleasure to your spouse</u>. Sex was created by God for two reasons. First, He wants us to procreate. Second, He wants us to experience pleasure in marriage. As we pursue giving and receiving pleasure in marriage, we need to feel free to explore the realms of sexual pleasure and to know where the boundaries are.

As I've taught and counseled on sex in marriage over the years, I have had many people ask me privately about what is allowed and not allowed sexually. In many cases, couples feel somewhat reluctant to experiment with certain things because they fear they will sin or do something wrong. Here are some of the common things people ask me about:

- Oral sex
- Using vibrators or sex toys
- Different sexual positions other than the missionary position
- Anal sex
- Acting out sexual fantasies

In addressing these issues with couples, I first of all tell them that God wants them to enjoy sex. Also, I tell them that when something isn't specifically forbidden in Scripture, it generally is because it is allowed. An example is oral sex. I've heard a good number of preachers over the years talk about how it is a sin. However, there is no place in Scripture where it is forbidden. The same guidelines apply to the other practices listed above. Although I am not necessarily endorsing or recommending them, I also don't believe a preacher or anyone else has the moral authority to tell a person what he or she can or cannot do in the privacy of their bedrooms if the Bible hasn't forbidden it.

Here are the important issues I believe you need to consider in allowing or disallowing any sexual practice:

- Is it forbidden in the Bible?
- Does it violate my conscience before God?
- Does it violate my spouse or is it against his or her will?
- Is this physically safe? Does it cause harm to me or my spouse? Are there health issues or risks involved?
- Does this treat my spouse in a disrespectful manner or damage our relationship?

These are the important questions to consider in helping you to find a place of resolving your sexual parameters. Again, let me emphasize that God wants you to have fun and enjoy sex. I believe there are broad parameters for sexual fulfillment in marriage, and if it feels good to you and isn't against God's Word, you should consider it. The best marriages are those in which two people enjoy each other and make each other feel good. It is important that you approach sex from this perspective and don't let the opinions of people dictate your sexual practices. You know better than anyone, except God, what you like and what is best for your marriage. When properly practiced, sex builds and bonds your relationship and creates an atmosphere of pleasure and delight.

Once you know how to resolve questions related to your sexual practices, it is important to put energy into pleasing your spouse. Remember, if men and women could fulfill themselves sexually, they wouldn't get married. Couples depend upon the creativity and energy of their spouses to meet their sexual needs. Even if they don't understand their spouses' sexual needs, it's important to value them. Also, many times in marriage, one spouse will have a desire for sex at times when the other doesn't. The temptation is to refuse their advances or to reluctantly participate. This can cause deep frustration and resentment.

Sexual fulfillment is experienced when two people are sensitive to one another and are committed to meeting each other's sexual needs in a creative and energetic manner. Never get lazy or take your spouse for granted. Find out what pleases him or her, and learn to give sexual pleasure to your spouse. The more you put into it, the more your marriage will benefit from your investment.

d.) <u>Find positive solutions to sexual problems</u>. There are seasons of marriage that bring with them special challenges. An example is when a woman's normal lubrication of her vagina during sex begins to dry up when she enters her late thirties and early forties. Because of this, she can begin to experience pain during sex. If an answer isn't found, a woman can begin to resist the sexual advances of her husband and actually dread sex. The answer to this issue is for a husband to use KY Jelly or another water-based lubricant during intercourse or in direct stimulation of his wife's clitoris. It replaces a woman's natural lubrication and restores the pleasure of sex without pain.

Also, as a man ages, he can have difficulty achieving erections. This is obviously a serious problem that requires a solution. With the discovery of drugs such as Viagra, there is no need for sexual dysfunction to keep any man from achieving erections and experiencing good sex for the rest of his life.

There are other issues that can negatively affect our sex lives, such as the fear of becoming pregnant, pregnancy, menopause, serious illness, or the loss of a loved one. Regardless of what challenge we are facing, it is important that we face it together and find a solution. Especially when a medical issue is involved, we need to consult a physician. When the issues are emotional or spiritual in nature, we need to get the help we need to keep our marriage as healthy as possible.

We must remember that even when we are facing a challenging time in life, our sexual needs and our spouses' needs don't necessarily go away. In a healthy marriage, sex is a constant current that ebbs and flows through our lives. Any time it stops for any significant period of time and for any reason, it must be dealt with as a serious problem that requires attention. Healthy marriages are marked by an attitude of sexual sensitivity and understanding. Every challenge or problem is met with an attitude of mutual concern and commitment to do what is best for the marriage.

I hope this booklet has helped you understand the important subject of sexual fulfillment in marriage. I pray you will be able to succeed in experiencing the greatest degree of sexual pleasure and fulfillment in your marriage. God bless you.

Recommended Reading

Intimate Issues by Linda Dillow and Lorraine Pintus (Waterbrook Press)

Intended for Pleasure by Ed and Gaye Wheat (Revell Publishing)